Options After High School

Steps to Success for College or Career

Lee Binz,
The HomeScholar

First Printing, 2015

Printed in the United States of America
Cover Design by Robin Montoya
Edited by Kimberly Charron

ISBN: 1511587245
ISBN-13: 978-1511587242

Options After High School

Steps to Success for College or Career

What are Coffee Break Books?

Options After High School is part of The HomeScholar's Coffee Break Book series.

Designed especially for parents who don't want to spend hours and hours reading a 400-page book on homeschooling high school, each book combines Lee's practical and friendly approach with detailed, but easy-to-digest information, perfect to read over a cup of coffee at your favorite coffee shop!

Never overwhelming, always accessible and manageable, each book in the series will give parents the tools they need to tackle the tasks of homeschooling high school, one warm sip at a time.

Everything about these Coffee Break Books is designed to connote simplicity, ease and comfort - from the size (fits in a purse), to the font and paragraph length (easy on the eyes), to the price (the same as a Starbucks Venti Triple Caramel Macchiato). Unlike a fancy coffee drink, however, these books are guilt-free pleasures you will want to enjoy again and again!

Table of Contents

Introduction

A College Prep Education is Important

High school can be like driving on auto-pilot. You arrive at the destination, but can't remember the journey! When you homeschool high school, sometimes life races by and your child is a senior before you know what happened!

College preparation is critical for students planning to attend college. College bound students need course work to prepare along with college admission tests, and parents need to learn about grades and credits

What can college preparation provide students who do *not* attend college?

Why bother getting your kids ready for college when you feel certain they won't go? Consider for a moment how many times your children have changed their mind. When you least expect it, on any topic, teenagers change their minds. Stop laughing! You know it's true! And teenagers may even change their minds about attending college.

Rigorous academics can benefit children even if they are not heading to college. When high school may be their only formal education, you want it to be the best! Focus on requirements for the college bound to ensure challenging academics. Excellence means keeping your children challenged, not achieving a prescribed level. Calculus does not make the difference between a college bound teen and a teen who doesn't attend college. Instead, learning how to learn is what prepares a child for college and for life.

Life would be much easier if our children made up their minds once and stuck to it! Unlike changing dinner plans from enchiladas to spaghetti, changing from vocational training to college preparation is more challenging. By planning a college prep high school education, you don't have to worry about changing plans. You and your student will be ready for anything. Prepare your children for college as part of your homeschool, taking to heart the Boy Scout motto, "Always be prepared."

Giving your child a college prep education is not complicated. You can continue to homeschool the same way you always have, learning with reckless abandon. You don't have to change your curriculum, or give tests in every subject, or chain your student to a desk. Homeschoolers of every stripe are successful with college admission. Don't change what has always worked for you; just set your eyes on college so you have the ultimate flexibility when your student graduates.

If you are stressed that your high school teen hasn't found a career interest yet, relax. Some kids decide on a career when they are still young and others don't decide until much later. Working adults change careers three to seven times in their lifetime! In the same way, it's not unusual for college students to change majors at least once in their college career. And even if your student chooses a career now, it's unlikely that they will continue with that career throughout their entire life. Live without regrets. Be prepared for anything, because with teenagers, anything can happen!

A Note about Teenagers

As your teen is growing up, remember they are also growing into adulthood. They are trying to become an adult and make adult decisions. Decision making skills don't appear overnight. Teens need practice. They want to become independent, and you want to encourage them to grow up.

This is that time in life when you should consider the five-year plan. When giving advice or direction, consider whether this will matter in five years. You can always give advice, but don't get too emotionally invested in children taking your advice unless it will matter in five years. Most of your suggestions won't matter in five years!

Chapter 1

Early Graduation

I sometimes get phone calls from parents asking whether they should graduate their child early since they've heard graduation requires only 24 credits. Their children may only be 16 years old and already have 24 credits. High school graduation occurs around 17 to 19 years old. It's difficult to tell if early graduation is a *good* idea, because it varies from family to family, child to child, college to college, and even year to year as your child matures! Your child can start high school early, or graduate early, or both.

I can tell you what worked for me. I waited until it was time to graduate my son, then I arranged the previous four years of education and called it high school. His final year became senior year, the year before was junior, and the year before was sophomore. He had already collected college credits, so he graduated high school at 16 and entered the university with credit for freshman year and started with junior year status. If you are confident that your homeschool transcript is honest and true, you can graduate your child early.

There are benefits and drawbacks of early graduation.

The benefits of graduating early:

- Get a head start on college or career.

- They can take college courses when eager and ready for them.

- Less *senioritis*.

- Busy students can focus on college applications during that busy time of life.

- They can graduate college earlier than their age-mates and enter the job force earlier.

The drawbacks of graduating early:

- The possibility of being overwhelmed by more mature students who are seeking a spouse or engaged in partying in college.

- Instead of excelling, your student may become a couch potato and experience failure to launch.

- Colleges or employers may see it as senioritis or a gap year.

- The student may be considered less mature and therefore less desirable by colleges and employers.

If you're just not sure that early graduation is right for your child, there are other things you can do to satisfy your child's needs.

Instead of graduating early:

- Keep curriculum challenging but not overwhelming.

- Consider homeschooling a few college classes with CLEP or AP tests.

- Your child can take a gap year.

- They can enter community college while living at home.

- Your child can take more high school credits than necessary to strengthen their application, so they can get into a more selective college as a much stronger applicant.

Regardless of what you decide, remember that your goal is to nurture your child into a self-supporting, independent adult.

Chapter 2

Community College Dual Enrollment

Community college dual enrollment is when your child takes community college classes while still in high school. This has become popular in homeschool circles—somewhat of a fad. Consider this option carefully. Don't just go with the crowd; do your own research.

Benefits of dual enrollment in community college:

- A way to gain great outside documentation of your child's homeschool education.

- Amazing letters of recommendation to include in

your child's comprehensive records, from college professors.

- Grades from an accrediting agency.

- Save money on tuition.

- Quickly earn missing credits from your child's high school transcript.

Drawbacks of community college dual enrollment include:

- Permanent grades—unlike classes in your homeschool, failure is a distinct option; it will be reported with university application.

- Community colleges tend to have lower academic requirements than other universities—classes are at a lower level.

- Keep in mind that community college can be a *rated R* environment.

- The worldview taught at the community college may not mesh with your family's.

- The same socialization issues that plague public high school can be found in a community college environment.

I'm not a big fan of community college dual enrollment, but I know that it makes sense in some situations. For a more detailed explanation on why I hesitate recommending dual enrollment, see my Coffee Break Book, *How to Homeschool College.*

If you decide that community college is the right path for your child, for maximum benefit:

- Plan a class in each core subject area: English, math, science, foreign language, history/geography, and fine arts. If your child works on an AA degree, they will cover all major subject areas, and more.

If you are using community college for one subject, that's great! Have your child take a required class at their favorite university. Some colleges require freshmen to take psychology, for instance.

- Find out each university's policy on community college classes. Universities may not accept college credits or may consider students transfer applicants instead of freshmen (which can affect scholarships).

- Keep records you normally provide for homeschool classes: transcript, course descriptions, reading list, activity and award list. Remember to save the college course descriptions for classes taken.

- Make sure your child gets excellent grades—hopefully all A's in college classes. Don't choose classes over their head. College grades are weighed heavily even if a university does not give you credit for them.

- Remind your student to get to know their professors, who can be great sources of letters of recommendation for college admission. Urge your child to sit in the front row, ask questions, and participate, so professors know them.

Chapter 3

Community College as an Adult

Once your child has graduated from homeschool and is 18 years old, should you send them to community college? It can be a little different when your child attends college as an adult—they can handle more adult situations. Adult decisions are different from those made by a young person; adults weigh the pros and cons more effectively.

One of the most wonderful things happened to my 18-year-old when he attended community college—he met his wife. I was surprised he could meet somebody so wonderful at community college. There are certainly some benefits to attending as an adult.

At a community college, your child can catch up in a subject quickly and go on to their first choice university. It can be particularly helpful for a student who had to be dragged kicking and screaming through homeschool graduation, but becomes an adult who is willing to learn. A motivated adult can easily transition into community college and get what they need.

Vocational training is also available at some community and vocational colleges. These are hands-on programs providing what your child might need to get an internship or a job. Community colleges can offer a special two-year degree that's called an AA or Associate of Arts degree. It's a relatively inexpensive option as well.

Regardless of how old your children are, it can help to see what others say about the community college you're considering. They will usually say the college was wonderful, but always listen to anything they say after "but." Then ask yourself whether it's what your child is ready for. Be careful that choices are not based on peer pressure and your child's friend's choice of college isn't the main consideration.

Chapter 4

Distance Learning

When I was younger, many students enjoyed distance learning—it's not a new phenomenon. Years ago, work was sent via snail mail. The company sent a packet of information, the student completed the work, filled out the test, mailed it back in, and earned a grade. The only difference now is that distance learning is electronic, which is much faster. Colleges are used to seeing distance learning on a transcript.

Your child can work on distance learning courses independently and then earn credit through testing. This involves taking CLEP or AP tests (www.collegeboard.com), or DSST tests (www.getcollegecredit.com). College policies vary, so make sure the program you choose will meet your child's needs.

My children learned through CLEP exams in our homeschool. It is possible to do so independently. We used *The CLEP Official Study Guide*. It includes study information and tests.

CLEP exams count as outside documentation of your homeschool, plus you might want to use CLEPs for college credit to save money. There are two basic ways of attaining credits through CLEP. One way is to follow behind your student and scoop up what they already know through all their reading, which is how I did it. I gave an assessment and if they passed, I gave them the study guide. When they passed the practice test in the study guide, I knew it was time for them to take the CLEP exam. My son loved economics and devoured any economics book. He received the highest possible score when he took the test for real.

The other way of preparing is to study the subject on purpose. Assign your child new material for a CLEP exam in a college subject. For example, my son did not want to study psychology at college. He did not want to learn about Freud in a room with girls. Instead, he used the study guide for psychology and read through it to get all the information he needed. He passed the sample test, so we took him in for the official CLEP which he passed 3wand never had to study psychology again.

Follow along behind and gather your child's college credits as they learn naturally, or your child can learn on purpose and earn specific college credits. The key is to be sure your child will pass the test before you register them.

Whichever way you decide to approach the CLEP, follow these steps:

- Find the policy for the college(s) you and your child are interested in.

- Decide on which exam.

- Find a test center and register.

- Study for the test.

You can also get professional help with distance education. I recommend Lumerit (getunbound.org), a good Christian organization that mentors students who are homeschooling college. This has real benefits as students can be difficult for their own parents to work with but not nearly as much trouble for other adults.

For more information on distance learning, check out:

- *Accelerated Distance Learning*

- *Bear's Guide to Earning Degrees* by Distance Learning

Chapter 5

Public University

University admission is a process, and a lengthy one at that. Application forms are like your 1040 forms for the IRS! The process will take up much of senior year, so start the application process on the first day!

Applications often require an application essay, which is a self-reflective, technically perfect essay written by your teenager. These essays can take quite a bit of time. Helping with editing is fine, but don't write the essay for them because college admission officers can tell when Mom and Dad have been too involved in the writing process.

For admission, you need letters of recommendation. When you ask somebody to write a letter of recommendation, allow plenty of time for them to complete it.

Financial aid forms need to be filled out as well! While public universities are funded by the government and don't have much scholarship money to give away, private universities do. With scholarships, private universities can be more cost-effective than public universities! Chances are your child will be able to earn scholarships if you apply early.

When applying for college, make sure your child includes *reach* colleges (challenging for them to get into), *fit* schools which your child is a perfect fit for, and *safety* schools in case they don't gain admission to the others. You also need to think about what it will be like for your teen to live at the public university you're considering. Many public universities offer a substance free dorm but find out what their definition of *substance free* is. A study for the University of Washington found that *only* 50% of the kids in the substance free dorm drink to excess on a regular basis. Substance free may not mean what you think it means.

Dorm life can cause culture shock. Visit to look around with your own eyes and see what's going on in that living environment. Attending college fairs and visiting colleges themselves are important steps to decide if a public university is right for your child.

Chapter 6

Private Christian College

Your child may require college because college diplomas are required for many jobs. My husband was an engineer for a large aerospace company. Somebody who attended college built the airplane you fly in. Before I was a homeschooling mom, I was a registered nurse working at a hospital to ensure people didn't die. Every time you go to the hospital, you're taken care of by people who attended college.

College plans can materialize out of nowhere. As a parent, you can forget that your child may have their own plan and mission for the future. If college didn't make sense for you, it's natural to think it won't be a fit for your child. Instead of focusing on your academic history, focus on providing flexibility for your student's academic future. You have to be careful to let them listen to their own call, and not to get it mixed up with your own desires. Be prepared for anything because you may want them to be a missionary, a nurse, or a stay-at-home mom, but God's calling may be different. Be prepared for anything so they're ready for anything God calls them to do.

Like families, Christian colleges aren't perfect. Keep in mind that the word some of the largest secular schools in the nation have *Christian* in their name. It can simply mean that 150 years ago a Christian founded the school, but it may not have been Christian in practice for the past 100 years. The flip side is that you may find a wonderful Christian college that doesn't have *Christian* in their name anywhere.

Regardless of the name, look carefully at each college to make sure it's an environment that matches your values as closely as possible. Consider whether you could live there as a Christian adult. Would you want to live in that environment and could you maintain your faith if you lived there for four years without your parents or family? Since it's impossible to tell by the name, you always need to visit.

When my own boys were applying to college, we had certain requirements. I wanted a Christian school that could minimize unwelcome socialization. I wanted a school within an hour drive of a family member in case of roommate disasters. For my youngest son, it had to be a college within driving distance from home so he could live at home until he was 18. My older son needed an engineering college, and he didn't want to leave Washington state.

I once heard a father boldly proclaim, "If your child can go to an Ivy League school, they *should* go to an Ivy League school." I disagree strongly. Only a parent knows where a child *should* go to college. While it's nice to have general ideas and apply to a variety of schools, there is simply not one right college for brilliant kids, or any child.

When my children applied to college, I had a tiny college fund. I knew they would be well qualified for a small private Christian college and would likely receive solid financial aid. At the same time, I knew that however smart they were, most of the applicants at Harvard and Yale would be just as smart—or smarter. The chances of financial aid would be slim and we needed quite a bit of financial aid.

When children are smart (or even geniuses), it's tempting to look toward an Ivy League school. Instead, I encourage parents to look at the *right* school. For some kids and families, this means avoiding well-ranked schools with great reputations. My children had near-perfect SAT scores but we didn't even apply to Stanford, Harvard, or Yale ... they weren't a fit for my family.

Parents know best. Know your child and trust yourself. Even if someone else thinks they know what is best for your child, this doesn't make it true. Only the mom and dad have *all* the details.

Chapter 7

Gap Year

In my day, taking time off between high school and college was almost unheard of—unless the student joined the military, the Peace Corps, or ran away to "find themselves." (That sounds more hip than saying, "Please Dad! Don't make me go to college!")

These days, taking a gap year is becoming more common, is favorable, and even seen as a benefit by some colleges. Children can do amazing things before college, and it's an option to consider.

What is a Gap Year?

A gap year usually lasts between six months and a year. During this time, the high school graduate works at a job or does volunteer work to gain experience before beginning their college career. Students are still considered freshmen unless they take a college course. Some colleges defer enrollment, which means the student is accepted and then waits a year to attend. Other schools will not defer enrollment.

Gap year policies vary. Some colleges consider students to be transfers if they take a gap year. Other colleges (including Ivy League colleges) will admit students, give great scholarships, encourage taking a gap year, and let students retain freshman status when they return! Unfortunately, any specific advice I give on gap years will be incomplete.

In the United Kingdom, most kids take a gap year after high school. Here, it's a bit more unusual and you don't hear of too many students taking a gap year. It is becoming increasingly common among homeschoolers, however.

Check Your College Policy

Your best bet it to contact three or four colleges your child would *most* like to attend and ask them specifically for gap year information. Keep in mind that policies can change. Also, be careful that the policy they quote you is *grandfathered* and will not change if your student leaves for a year!

If your student is considering a gap year, fill out the applications as usual. Provide a transcript, reading lists, and course descriptions. Students who do not apply as a senior could be treated as a transfer student and miss out on many freshman scholarships. So, have your student apply while they are still in high school.

In one of the application essays, they should focus on their gap year plans and what they hope to accomplish.

While your student completes the application and essay, you can call colleges to research their policies. Make sure you visit each college, and have your student talk face to face with the admission department. That's as good as an interview and can go a long way to proving they are taking a gap year and accomplishing something.

Fill out the FAFSA. Colleges base their financial aid on the FAFSA, and (with luck) that financial aid decision will carry over once they return. You don't want your child to come back with college admission but not be able to afford the college.

A gap year is not usually affected by dual enrollment college courses. Include the community college course on the high school transcript for dual enrollment, to prove that it is not only a college class. College classes taken *after* high school graduation are the only ones that will mess up your child's gap year. Your student can take anything before graduation but nothing after graduation (no classes during the gap year).

Gap Year Experiences

Gap years are more common in other countries. Dorothy lives in the United Kingdom, and she says it's common there.

> There are hundreds of organizations which offer gap year experiences, mostly abroad. Christian kids tend to do missions work with people like YWAM. Rich kids will sometimes just go traveling. Some will go working through another country. We have two different young friends in Queensland at the moment, one working in Brisbane to see the country, another with YWAM (Youth

With a Mission). The way it works is you apply to university and once accepted you simply defer the place for a year. Discussing what you plan to do during your Gap Year or putting it in your application gives useful insight into your personality to the university. It's all automatic.

A gap year can work out well for two types of students. One student might still need maturing before attending to the trials of university life. Another may have a passionate interest in a subject and would like to acquire real-world experience in it. Both types of students need to be self-motivated or the year might end up being a waste. You don't want a gap year turning into a "couch potato year." If you think it could fit your family, discuss gap year options with your student first. Pursue it with colleges if there is any interest.

There are many advantages of a gap year:

- Colleges such as Harvard, Princeton, and Yale favor gap years.

- A gap year can give a child more time to mature before heading off to university, which will hopefully mean they have better focus (and be less likely to engage in wild partying).

- Sometimes a gap year can make all the difference between your child falling into the wrong crowd and being mature enough to succeed and seize the day.

- Your child can engage in meaningful activities they may not have time for with a rigorous curriculum and extracurricular activities.

You want your student to do something during their gap year, not be a couch potato. Community service, missionary work, volunteering, working at church, or good, old-fashioned work experience are all valuable experiences. Your child could search for scholarships while engaging in these meaningful activities.

Gap Year Resources

- Thinking Beyond Borders

thinkingbeyondborders.org

- Do Something.com

www.dosomething.org

- Harvest Ministry

harvestministry.org

- USA Gap Year Fairs

usagapyearfairs.org

Chapter 8

Work or Internships

College isn't the only path after graduation. Consider whether the right thing for your child is to launch directly into the working world.

Internships are a popular option for homeschoolers! They allow your child to try out a profession they might like to take on. Even unpaid internships are excellent for the experience. They may lead full-time jobs or at least great letters of recommendation.

Your child can develop entrepreneurial skills by running their own business or working for someone else. These are great ways for kids to learn about themselves and their abilities. One of my close friend's sons had learning disabilities and did not want to attend college. He started working at Starbucks after graduating from homeschool. After a couple of months, he realized that he was the smartest person in the workplace and that he had a lot to offer. This inspired him to earn a business degree. He went to college and graduated, despite his learning disabilities. When kids get out into the working world, it can give them the confidence needed to take the next step.

Provide the best possible education in your homeschool, because you don't know which skills your child will need. For example, the young man who earned a business degree required math because he needed to take accounting classes. The planning they did ahead of time prepared him for anything he wanted to pursue.

Even in families where women generally do not work outside the home, girls need a vocation to be fulfilled. Nobody feels satisfied sitting on a couch all day, and everybody needs to feel productive. When these girls graduate, they need to provide full-time contributions of work in the home. Homeschool must prepare them for marriage and family, and the possibility of living independently if marriage doesn't follow graduation. The need for meaningful work is deeply embedded in all people and you need to encourage your child to find work to help them feel fulfilled.

One of my friends in Texas talks to her children about whether they want to be on the college track or on the work track in her homeschool. She told me that her college track is a lot easier than her working world track. When it's the college track, she knows they're heading to college and all those gaps will be filled. But the buck stops with her and she has to cover everything on the vocational track. Her son applied to a public university and was admitted within one week's time! She had no idea he applied because he was living on his own. He was determined to be a manager and when it required a business degree, he knew he had to apply for college. She was glad she had made her vocational track so thorough!

Chapter 9

Join the Military

Good news for homeschoolers who want to enlist in the army upon graduation: they can!

In the past, it may have been a detriment. Years ago, homeschoolers were put on par with high school dropouts when applying to enlist in the army, and they required a GED. Why? Because the best predictor of a student's likelihood of adapting to the military is a traditional high school diploma. Now, enlistment parameters have changed.

Today homeschoolers are *Tier 1* recruits like their public schooled peers. Many students with an alternative education have been successful in the military.

I joined the Army National Guard as a junior in high school. I was seventeen. And I was, you guessed it, homeschooled! The recruiters I worked with couldn't believe that I was self-motivated, which comes naturally after being homeschooled; I was able to fill out paperwork quickly and correctly. And most of all, they couldn't believe how easy it was for me to pass a background check. I qualified for a Top Secret security clearance (which due to medical issues, I never ended up using). I had never done marijuana, been convicted of a felony, and was able to provide every reference they asked for. Weird, right?

My homeschool education *absolutely* prepared me to pass the ASVAB with an extremely high score, and I was offered a job designation in the field that I wanted (intelligence). I had to laugh, though, because my scores also qualified me for a mechanic position; I am the least mechanically minded person I know! If your child is called to serve this great country, please know that being homeschooled might just make him an excellent candidate.

~ Laura

According to the www.goarmy.com website:

Homeschoolers must possess a home-school diploma and submit transcripts at the time of enlistment. The course work must involve parental supervision, the transcript must reflect the normal credit hours per subject used in a traditional high school and the diploma must be issued in compliance with applicable state laws.

Take the Armed Services Vocational Aptitude Battery test. The Armed Forces Qualification Test score from the ASVAB will determine enlistment eligibility.

Must take the Assessment of Individual Motivation test, which is 20-minute pencil-and-paper test. The AIM test score is used to obtain data and does not affect qualification for enlistment.

At a minimum, the last academic year (9 months) must be completed in a home-school environment.

The Army also offers enlistment cash bonuses to homeschool graduates, providing they score high enough. They get the same incentives as traditional high school graduates, including up to

$40,000 for enlistments lasting three years or more.

Scoring well on the ASVAB test is important. Look up practice tests on the internet, or have your child take classes at a local center to prepare.

If your child is thinking of joining the military upon high school graduation, consider a military academy or ROTC scholarships in college. Homeschoolers can be eligible for these opportunities.

Military Academy and ROTC

As you are guiding your child through college preparation, research the ROTC program. ROTC stands for "Reserve Officer Training Corps"—a college program offered at many universities that prepares young adults to become officers in the U.S. Military. In exchange for a paid college education and a guaranteed post-college career, cadets commit to serve in the Military after graduation, so don't take this lightly—

it's serious business. ROTC representatives attend college fairs, so you can research this option as you are looking for colleges.

Let me stand back and let another mom tell you the good news about homeschoolers getting into military academies. Here are real tips from a real mom with experience! Thanks for sharing, Cassie!

Hi Lee,

Now that we are nearing the end of the year I wanted to update you on Sara's plans for next year.

Sara was fortunate to receive a nomination to the U.S. Naval Academy from our representative and a nomination to the U.S. Air Force Academy from one of our senators. Unfortunately, she did not receive an appointment to either school, although she was qualified in every area. We are so very proud of her accomplishments and more importantly her tenacity.

Sara also applied for an Air Force ROTC scholarship and received a full tuition scholarship! These are also quite hard to come by (15,000 applicants, 4,000 qualified candidates, and 911 scholarships offered in 2011) so that is her plan B. She was accepted at Miami University in Oxford, OH, as well as Ohio State university, and received merit scholarships from both schools. At this point, she is leaning towards attending Miami and with her combined scholarships school will be paid for!

Thanks again for all of your help and support over the last few years! It is hard to believe that we are "shutting the doors" on our little homeschool. We are so very proud of Sara and all of her hard work. We are also so proud of her determination to serve our country and look forward to her commissioning in four years.

There are several things I would share with parents about this entire process. Obviously, first I would tell them to use all the resources that you have made available! Seriously! While I had always kept good records, you really helped me put it all together in a very concise, readable, and professional way.

As far as applying to the academies and for ROTC scholarships, my first piece of advice would be to make sure it is completely student driven. I honestly did very little except to send records and letters of recommendation when Sara asked me to do so. I did not keep up with due dates or anything!

If a young person has a desire to serve as an officer, then they have to show the initiative and go through many interviews with congressional staff members, liaison officers and ROTC commanders. Being a *helicopter parent* is definitely a no-no at this point.

I did have contact with the academic counselor at the Air Force Academy as she needed some clarification for a class that Sara had taken at a small private school (with no school profile!) and she commented on the quality and thoroughness of Sara's records. For the academies and ROTC a transcript will not suffice. Even members of congress require school documents with the nomination applications! I had to send detailed course descriptions and lists of textbooks we had used so it is best to keep up with this on a yearly basis so you can just pull it together at the end.

Also, be prepared to write letters for your own child! I would have never thought that anyone would want me to do so but all of the academies, ROTC, and our senators and representatives each requested this. It was initially difficult but I remembered what you had said to me about describing how mastery of subjects had guided our decisions, and that helped to focus my remarks. I also think it is important to think of one quality about your child and describe how that is demonstrated by your child's accomplishments. I focused on Sara's quality of tenacity (in abundance since birth!) and how she simply never gave up even if she initially had failed at something . . . like when she didn't get into our city's competitive youth orchestra on the first try. She was hurt and disappointed but practiced harder and got in the next year.

Once Sara received the ROTC scholarship, we have accompanied her on visits to detachments and the officers are very friendly and that's when you can become more involved. But ride in the *back seat* until then. The commander of the Miami University detachment shared with us that his top two cadets in the detachment were homeschooled and he is very excited to have Sara join them.

I hadn't thought about canceling my membership, but I guess it is time for that. Makes me sad. You have really made a difference in our lives and helped two young people achieve their dreams by helping their mom, so our family thanks you from the bottom of our hearts!

~ Cassie

I heard from Cassie with an update on her daughter.

For those students who really want to attend one of the military academies, don't give up hope. Sara had accepted her ROTC scholarship and was set to activate it at Miami University when she received an email in the middle of May asking if she would be interested in accepting a Falcon Foundation Scholarship from the U.S. Air Force Academy to attend one of eight military prep schools this year, and then matriculate at the academy in June 2013. Virtually all students who take this path are admitted, so she jumped at the opportunity!

She must go through the nomination process again but the Academy application is very simple this year. All of the academies have similar programs, so don't be discouraged if an appointment is not offered the first year. In fact, many academy students apply while in college and participating in ROTC. Students can enter the academy until the age of 21 so if it is a dream, be tenacious.

See Appendix 2 for more resources for Military Prep in High School.

The sky's the limit!

Chapter 10

The Couch Potato Strategy

The goal of graduating your child is to graduate an independent adult. If they're not sitting on the couch, then life is good. But if they are on the couch all the time, then their potential is wasted. How do you prevent this from happening?

It's all about setting expectations. When your child is around 16, you can expect them to work during the summer. It's one of the ways they can develop a work ethic and learn what it is like to work for a living. Teach them to work hard in whatever career they choose.

Your goal is for them to be independent. You're working your way out of your parenting and teaching job, not trying to get them to live under your roof forever. Remember that God has a call on their life like God has a plan for your own life.

If your teen hasn't found their calling yet, you can help by being their guidance counselor and helping them explore career options. There are so many jobs out there that your child may not have thought about or even heard of before! Here are books and resources I recommend for career guidance.

1. Larry Burkett's series

- *Your Career in Changing Times*

- *Finding the Career That Fits You: The Companion Workbook to Your Career in Changing Times*

This book and workbook are from a Christian perspective.

2. What Color is Your Parachute

- *What Color Is Your Parachute? A Practical Manual for Job-Hunters and Career-Changers*

3. Websites and Information about Career Exploration

- www.quickstart.collegeboard.org/posweb/login.jsp
  My College QuickStart by the College Board offers a free personality test for identifying your child's strengths and provides college major and career suggestions

- www.humanmetrics.com
  Personality tests, some free

- http://www.bls.gov/ooh
  Occupational Outlook Handbook free e-book

- www.careerkey.org
  Personality related to occupations ($9.95)

- www.thecallonline.com
  The Call Vocational and Life Purpose Guide from Focus on the Family ($100)

- www.careerdirectonline.org
  Career Direct assessment from Crown Financial Ministries, founded by Larry Burkett ($80)

If your child is undecided about college or career, consider enrolling them in a liberal arts college. At a liberal arts college, students take classes in a wide variety of subjects. The first two years of the exploratory curriculum usually include science, social sciences (psychology for example), English, and politics. Exposure to a varied curriculum helps students explore many subjects and eventually they will find areas they love.

If nothing grabs them, graduates of liberal arts schools still graduate with a general liberal arts degree. Many businesses look on these degrees favorably. Most train all their new employees and simply want an employee with *any* bachelor's degree. Liberal Arts can provide good preparation for many jobs.

If you've done everything and nothing seems to help get your young adult off the couch, check these resources out:

- Find encouragement in the article, "Parenting Super Hero or Not?" from Crosswalk

- *Setting Boundaries with Your Adult Children: Six Steps to Hope and Healing for Struggling Parents* by Allison Bottke

- *Parenting Your Adult Child: How you can help them achieve their full potential* by Campbell and Chapman

- *When Our Grown Kids Disappoint Us: Letting Go of*

Their Problems, Loving Them Anyway, and Getting on with Our Lives by Jane Adams

It's difficult when your child has no plans. The whole *what's next* thing is much like a wedding. Wedding plans do not take care of themselves and the same is true for what happens after graduation. Think about it and talk about it openly with your child.

Conclusion

Letting Go

Children will grow up and there's nothing you can do about it. My children grew up, and I guarantee your children will grow up, too.

All these choices, except the couch potato, are valid and you shouldn't consider any as "bad" or "wrong." Each family is different, and each child has different needs. We have tremendous freedom when homeschooling high school, but also tremendous responsibility to make wise decisions together with our children. 20/20 hindsight is great, but what we're attempting is foresight. It may not be perfect and we may make missteps, but there are real advantages to carefully considering and praying about your child's options.

Regardless of what you choose, it is extremely helpful if you prepare a transcript and a diploma for your child. At some point, someone will ask your child whether they have a high school transcript and you want them to say "yes." Even if they don't ask to see the transcript, sometimes they want to know it exists. Once you have completed your child's homeschool transcript, keep it in your safe deposit box, back it up on your computer, and email it to yourself so you can access it later from a different computer.

It's the same for the diploma. In a job interview, they'll ask whether your child is a high school graduate and whether they have a high school diploma. You want them to say "yes" without hesitation, not "No, I was only homeschooled."

Letting Go . . . to College

I was a little surprised by this article in the New York Times. What an unfriendly title: *Students, Welcome to College; Parents, Go Home.*

> As the latest wave of superinvolved parents delivers its children to college, institutions are building into the day, normally one of high emotion, activities meant to punctuate and speed the separation. It is part of an increasingly complex process, in the age of Skype and twice-daily texts home, in which colleges are urging "Velcro parents" to back off so students can develop independence.

I remember sending my children to college—both at once. Saying goodbye was emotional, but mostly I felt proud.

I notice that my close friends are dealing with children going off to college, and the letting go stage is so difficult! I want to encourage you to remember your goal to raise a successful adult. One day, you will also let go of your child! Take it one step at a time, but remember that this is an important job you are doing. So, I say, "Good job! What you are doing is important, and I'm proud of you for all the hard work!"

It is okay for your child to leave home when they become an adult! 1 Corinthians 13:11 says:

> When I was a child, I spoke like a child, I thought like a child, and I reasoned like a child. But when I became a man, I gave up my childish ways.

There will be a time when your child is ready to be an adult. Remember, there is a big difference between a newborn and a 4-year-old, and there's almost the same difference between a 14-year-old and 18-year-old. There are also four years between an 18-year-old and a 22-

year-old. A night and day difference exists between each of those four-year spans.

Parting Advice

When sending your children off into the world, I want to repeat the two most important pieces of advice. If you forget everything else you've read, please remember this. It will save you from lots of stress and heartache:

1. Keep your five year plan in mind. In five years, you want to have a happy, healthy, close extended family. When conflict occurs during college, keep your five year plan in mind.

2. Step in only when kids are being life-threateningly stupid. They will make poor choices, but they can learn from them like you and I do every day. The only time you need to step in is when they are being dangerously dumb. Believe me . . . it happens, not often, but it happens.

When you are done homeschooling, will you be able to move forward, without regrets? Take a deep breath and be calm. Remember that your goal is to raise an adult who will go out into society and make the world a better place. The rest of their education is merely for bonus points.

Appendix 1

Choose Your Battles

Teenagers. The word can make adults shudder! Often the mere mention of the word is accompanied by a head shake or a groan. But it doesn't have to be that way. A little understanding and choosing your battles can go a long way when dealing with your teenager in your homeschool!

Resistance is Futile

Resistance can look like many things in teenagers—from refusing to put on a coat when asked, to bringing home a big can of worms, their resistance to our common-sense approach can be so frustrating! When our children are young, sometimes parents work hard to train children that resistance is futile—simply obey Mom and Dad! But when teenagers get older, we realize that *our* resistance is futile. They often won't do what we ask; it's like leading a horse to water—you can't make them drink!

Trying to be an Adult

When your teen is growing up, remember they are also growing into adulthood. They are trying hard to become an adult and make adult decisions. Decision making doesn't happen overnight. They need practice. They want to become independent, and you want to encourage your teen to grow up.

Five Year Plan

When giving advice or direction, consider whether it will matter in five years. You can always give advice, but don't get too emotionally invested in your child taking your advice unless it will matter in five years. Most parental suggestions won't matter in five years at all.

Personal Preference

Independent adults are unique individuals with personal preferences, and your child is becoming an adult with their own unique interests, habits, and desires. As they get older, try not to step in if they are doing something due to personal preference. These are things you might see another adult doing and think "I wouldn't do it that way, but whatever!" That's how you know it's a personal preference—if you wouldn't confront a neighbor about it, you may not need to confront your child.

Life Threateningly Stupid

On the other hand, do try to step in when it's life-threatening or "life-threateningly stupid" as my husband and I would say. For example, when a blizzard is expected in Montana, it might be life-threateningly stupid to leave home without a coat, but usually it won't matter in five years. Most teenagers, especially older teens, are trying to make their own decisions. They need to face the consequences of their decisions so they can learn. If a decision won't hurt or matter in five years, and another adult might make the same decision without you intervening, then perhaps they need to learn by making that decision.

Life Alteringly Stupid

There are other decisions that may not cost their lives, but they can ruin their lives. In our society, premarital sex, alcohol abuse, and drug use are common examples. Some decisions are permanent and can't be taken back. Decisions about tattoos, for example, are life-altering (although not everyone thinks they are stupid, of course!) and it might be best to delay those decisions until adulthood, just to be sure.

Learning from Discomfort

When they make choices you wish they wouldn't, it may cause discomfort. I remember when Kevin wanted to take engineering classes *and* honors level courses in college. Ouch! That sounded painful! But when a decision will cause discomfort, your child may learn to avoid that discomfort when possible—and not volunteer to do something unnecessary or unimportant. When our children were two years old, I focused on natural consequences so they could see the results of disobedience. With teenagers, focus again on those natural consequences so they can learn.

Practice Making Decisions

Now is the best time to allow decision-making practice. You can help them consider their options (it may sound like advice to them, I suppose) and support them in their decision, even if you wouldn't make the same decision yourself. You can help them learn from their decisions as well—pointing out both the good and bad things they learned. Allow perfectly fine decisions, personal preferences, and a decision that another adult might choose to make even if you and I wouldn't make the same decision.

Appendix 2

Military Prep in High School

Let's be honest. Some kids would *love* to serve our country and want to start *today*. There are ways to encourage delight directed learning and their vocational calling while your child is still homeschooling. Each branch of the military has a high school experience, so see what is available in your area. All these programs emphasize life skills valuable for every student. Students can gain skills such as leadership, confidence, and discipline, which are necessary to be successful in any career.

Check out these options to see if they might be a good fit for your child.

- **U.S. Army JROTC**

www.usarmyjrotc.com

- **Civil Air Patrol - United States Air Force Auxiliary**

www.gocivilairpatrol.com

- **U.S. Naval Sea Cadet Corps**

www.seacadets.org

- **Young Marines**

www.youngmarines.com

There are other military experiences that can prepare for these kinds of careers.

- **Law Enforcement Explorer Program**

http://www.golawenforcement.com/ PoliceExplorer.htm

- **Boy Scouts of America: Eagle Rank**

www.scouting.org

- **College ROTC basics**

http://todaysmilitary.com/training/

Afterword

Who is Lee Binz and What Can She Do for Me?

Number one best-selling homeschool author, Lee Binz is The HomeScholar. Her mission is "helping parents homeschool high school." Lee and her husband, Matt, homeschooled their two boys, Kevin and Alex, from elementary through high school.

Upon graduation, both boys received four-year, full tuition scholarships from their first choice university. This enables Lee to pursue her dream job—helping parents homeschool their children through high school.

On The HomeScholar website, you will find great products for creating homeschool transcripts and comprehensive records to help you amaze and impress colleges.

Find out why Andrew Pudewa, Founder of the Institute for Excellence in Writing says, "Lee Binz knows how to navigate this often confusing and frustrating labyrinth better than anyone."

You can find Lee online at:

HomeHighSchoolHelp.com

If this book has been helpful, could you please take a minute to write us a quick review on Amazon? Thank you!

Testimonials

I love how you give specific directions and steps

Lee - again I feel refreshed just having someone to guide me along the way. I love how you give specific directions & steps. Thank you for being a blessing of encouragement in my life.

Grace & Peace,

~Dee in Texas

I feel so relieved!

Again, just 20 minutes with you and I feel so relieved! This "high school" thing is gonna be alright! Thanks for the list of books. Reading is the love language of both of my boys also. So, I truly appreciate this to give me a foundation. Thanks for everything you do.

~Annie in Florida

So many of my questions have been dissolved!

You have provided so much helpful information so many of my questions have been dissolved. I want to put into practice many of the things I have learned so far over the summer.

I now am a more confident retired GM dad overseeing my two sons learning choices knowing that The HomeScholar is a mouse click away! Thank you again for the quantity and quality of information you are providing to homeschoolers.

~Raymond in Michigan

For more information about my **Comprehensive Record Solution** and **Gold Care Club**, go to:

www.ComprehensiveRecordSolution.com
www.GoldCareClub.com

Also From The HomeScholar...

- The HomeScholar Guide to College Admission and Scholarships: Homeschool Secrets to Getting Ready, Getting In and Getting Paid (Book and Kindle Book)

- Setting the Records Straight—How to Craft Homeschool Transcripts and Course Descriptions for College Admission and Scholarships (Book and Kindle Book)

- TechnoLogic: How to Set Logical Technology Boundaries and Stop the Zombie Apocalypse

- Finding the Faith to Homeschool High School

- Total Transcript Solution (Online Training, Tools and Templates)

- Comprehensive Record Solution (Online Training, Tools and Templates)

- High School Solution (Online Training, Tools and Templates)

- College Launch Solution (Online Training, Tools, Templates and Support)

- Gold Care Club (Comprehensive Online Support and Training)

- Silver Training Club (Online Training)

- Parent Training A la Carte (Online Training)

The HomeScholar Coffee Break Books Released or Coming Soon on Kindle and Paperback:

- Delight Directed Learning: Guiding Your Homeschooler Toward Passionate Learning

- Creating Transcripts for Your Unique Child: Help Your Homeschool Graduate Stand Out from the Crowd

- Beyond Academics: Preparation for College and for Life

- Planning High School Courses: Charting the Course Toward High School Graduation

- Graduate Your Homeschooler in Style: Make Your Homeschool Graduation Memorable

- Keys to High School Success: Get Your Homeschool High School Started Right!

- Getting the Most Out of Your Homeschool This Summer: Learning just for the Fun of it!

- Finding a College: A Homeschooler's Guide to Finding a Perfect Fit

- College Scholarships for High School Credit: Learn and Earn With This Two-for-One Strategy!

- College Admission Policies Demystified: Understanding Homeschool Requirements for Getting In

- A Higher Calling: Homeschooling High School for Harried Husbands (by Matt Binz, Mr. HomeScholar)

- Gifted Education Strategies for Every Child: Homeschool Secrets for Success

- College Application Essays: A Primer for Parents

- Creating Homeschool Balance: Find Harmony Between Type A and Type Zzz...

- Homeschooling the Holidays: Sanity Saving Strategies and Gift Giving Ideas

- Your Goals this Year: A Year by Year Guide to Homeschooling High School

- Making the Grades: A Grouch-Free Guide to Homeschool Grading

- High School Testing: Knowledge That Saves Money

- Getting the BIG Scholarships: Learn Expert Secrets for Winning College Cash!

- Easy English for Simple Homeschooling: How to Teach, Assess and Document High School English

- Scheduling—The Secret to Homeschool Sanity: Plan You Way

Back to Mental Health

- Junior Year is the Key to High School Success: How to Unlock the Gate to Graduation and Beyond

- Upper Echelon Education: How to Gain Admission to Elite Universities

- How to Homeschool College: Save Time, Reduce Stress and Eliminate Debt

- Homeschool Curriculum That's Effective and Fun: Avoid the Crummy Curriculum Hall of Shame!

- Comprehensive Homeschool Records: Put Your Best Foot Forward to Win College Admission and Scholarships

- Options After High School: Steps to Success for College or Career

- How to Homeschool 9th and 10th Grade: Simple Steps for Starting Strong!

- Senior Year Step-by-Step: Simple Instructions for Busy Homeschool Parents

- How-to-Homeschool Independently: Do-it-Yourself Secrets to Rekindle the Love of Learning

- High School Math The Easy Way: Simple Strategies for Homeschool Parents in Over Their Heads

- Homeschooling Middle School with Powerful Purpose: How to Successfully Navigate 6th through 8th Grade

- Simple Science for Homeschooling High School: Because Teaching Science isn't Rocket Science!

Would you like to be notified when we offer the next Coffee Break Books for FREE during our Kindle promotion days? If so, leave your name and email below and we will send you a reminder.

HomeHighSchoolHelp.com/
freekindlebook

Visit my Amazon Author Page!

amazon.com/author/leebinz

Made in the USA
Las Vegas, NV
19 January 2022

41844531R00059